The
Unspoken
Dialogue

Understanding Body Language
and Controlling
Interviews and Negotiations

What People Are Saying...

A very useful tool to understand non-verbal language . . .
                    Norbert Reiss
                    Germany

Robert Rail is consummate in conveying the meaning of a universally recognized basic language - *body language* - which few, if any, give any thought to at any given time . . .
                    Officer Ruma Bhattacharji
                    India

This book is so instructive that wherever you are in the world you can pick it up and start instructing. It is applicable in any language or culture. A multi-lingual masterpiece!
                    Per Ersgard
                    Sweden

This material is a result of his hard work in the service for peace . . . mastery in body signs.
                    Evgueni Olmeltchenko
                    Russia

This is obviously the culmination of great experience and knowledge . . . As a lecturer he was as outstanding as the book.
                    Ali Abdel Halim
                    Jordan

Bob's knowledge of human behavior and his experience as a police officer combine to formulate "Body Signs" . . . it has been enjoyed and understood around the world.
                    Graham Ridding
                    ITSS - United Nations

What People Are Saying...

It was magnificent . . . Outstanding topic of great need! . . .
Francois Vigneron
France

After having been with the Danish Police Force for over twenty years I still learned a lot from Mr. Rail's teaching!
Steen Fleusborg
Denmark

There is always the hue and cry from political aspirants about minimum force . . . In the end, the Law Enforcement officers and their employers become liable victims. Thanks to Bob Rail, employer's financial liability levels will be greatly reduced. It would be wise for agencies to include the techniques in this book in their training package.
Augustine Sewoatsri
Ghana

The Unspoken Dialogue

Understanding Body Language
and Controlling
Interviews and Negotiations

by Robert R. Rail

VARRO PRESS
Kansas City

The *Unspoken* Dialogue
Understanding Body Language and Controlling Interviews and Negotiations

Robert R. Rail

VARRO PRESS
P.O. Box 8413
Shawnee Mission, Kansas 66208 USA
TEL: 913-385-2034 – FAX: 913-385-2039
WEB: www.varropress.com

Printed and bound in the United States of America

Rail, Robert R.
    The unspoken dialogue : understanding body language and
controlling interviews and negotiations / by Robert R. Rail. – 1st ed.
    p. cm.
    LCCN: 00-134766
    ISBN: 1-888644-16-8

    1. Body language. 2. Negotiation in business.
3. Employment interviewing.   I. Title.

BF637.N66R35 2001   153.6'9
                        QBI00-500164

Table of Contents

Foreword

I met Bob Rail in Bosnia and attended the first presentation he made about "body language"; I was impressed. He cast some light on a series of problems which had been bugging me for a while. I was in Bosnia as a political officer for the UN. I had to deal with many difficult mediation and negotiation situations. I was an experienced field officer who had directed the activities of others, both in and after conflict.

What was bugging me was the "culture gap". The most obvious manifestation of which was the absolutely sincere dishonesty of all the parties I dealt with. None of them were completely dishonest all the time. They all had a fairly quickly identifiable party line of rhetoric. But consistently, they confused and tricked us. Simply put, we didn't understand them. We heard the words but couldn't read the whole message. One vital set of clues which could have helped us was "body language", just to sort out what the real agenda items were - just to identify the real group leaders - just to reinforce our own message.

The more I got to know about body language, the more I thought of my other experiences in the navy. I had eight years service in submarines. Today, the most sophisticated listening devices are used to detect and then analyze sounds in the ocean. By a combination of previous intelligence and comparing characteristics, the sounds of enemy submarines can be sorted out from many other sounds in the ocean - SOMETIMES!! One thing that any submarine hunter will tell you is "we get a lot of false alarms". You would be surprised at the number of sea creatures that can make noises identical to one part of a "submarine signature". What we always wanted was more information from another sensor to corroborate our acoustic data. Sometimes, if we were lucky, a patrolling aircraft using its radar would get a brief detection on something metallic that suddenly disappeared. We could correlate this information with our unconfirmed acoustic data and BINGO! - a submarine which had come up to the surface for a quick look was caught! Once we had this independent corroboration, life was so much easier.

It's the same with body language. A difficult negotiator is a "tough nut", which ever culture they come from. You need to gather all the clues. You need to pin your suspect down. Words are important, but rarely enough, even when you are operating in your own culture, let alone an alien one.

A big part of using all the signals is to adopt the attitude of what radio guys call "a wide ban scanner". Just relax and take in everything. Listen, Look, Sense and don't be too quick to jump to conclusions. Gradually, if you stay open to all the signals, the correct picture will present itself. You're listening carefully to what someone is saying; you're noticing all their movements, big and small; you're controlling yourself to not give off any hostile signals. Slowly, your senses, more than your purely rational mind, tells you, "this is a lie", or "they don't believe this themselves but have to say it", . . . You have changed from purely receiving signals to analyzing and being able to take action.

Body language is not a brilliant, new revelation. Naturals have been doing it for centuries. All great communicators, both good and bad, have done it. If you look at film sequences of the great orators of the past, they used effective body language to control and direct their message. Using body language, both in reading others and reinforcing your own, will not, on its own, make you a millionaire. Body language is a super tool to use in all aspects of life to make you more effective, even if it only produces a small improvement. In many situations, the competitive edge will rely on this small margin. This is what fluency in body language can do for you.

If you are able to take in the common sense principles that are set out in this book, you will become a more effective communicator. You will be able to use these skills on both "offense" and "defense". Your personal relationship will benefit, you can consolidate work performance, and just feel more in control of your life.

> Graham Day
> Chief of Civil Affairs
> United Nations
> Sarajevo, Bosnia and
> Herzegovina

About the Author

R obert Rail has an outstanding background of over a quarter of a century of both combative martial arts knowledge and "on the street" law enforcement experience. He is an internationally respected and acclaimed master instructor to nations and universities around the world. As an expert witness and advisor, Bob is highly regarded by legal and judicial professionals. His widely acclaimed text *Defense Without Damage* is available through practically every law enforcement catalog and professional source. His many tactical training sessions have been aired on both educational and cable television networks. In addition, Bob serves as a writer and advisor to numerous law enforcement magazines and journals.

During his two tours of duty in a war zone as an officer with the United Nations International Peace Keeping Force, Bob had the responsibility and honor of instructing and designing curriculums for the elite officers of the 44 nations that were deployed through Bosnia. He was also physical confrontation advisor and resource provider to select NATO units and personnel.

Through all his classes, lectures, presentations, and even casual contacts, Bob Rail displays a constant flow of encouragement, enthusiasm, and instructional humor. As a member of the Martial Arts Hall of Fame, United Nations

International Police Task Force, and as director of training for Hiatt-Thompson Corporation, you will be aware of only one thing when you meet Bob. He is now, and always will be, a friend to the men and women of law enforcement throughout the world.

Charles E. Thompson
President
Hiatt-Thompson Corporation

Introduction

Regardless of where a person comes from or what verbal language they speak, they send a very clear message to us without ever uttering a sound. The position of their body, and the placement and use of their arms, legs, head, and eyes all can give us insight into this person beyond the conversation taking place in front of us. If we know how to interpret these messages from the body, it can greatly affect our ability to understand not only the message of their words, but also the significance of what their body is saying.

We all use signals from people who cannot speak, such as infants or people who are ill or injured, and never give it a second thought. Too often, we forget about or ignore these signs when dealing with people who can speak. To fully understand what is taking place in front of us, we need to comprehend the total dialogue being presented, not just the spoken words.

This manual will help you understand and evaluate the nonverbal messages of those with whom we routinely contact, and those we encounter in the day-to-day situations that occur as part of our regular job activities. It will also provide us with some valuable information as to what we can do in an interview, meeting, or negotiation, whether it is a one on one, or in a group, to ensure our body language is allowing us to maintain control.

Part One

Body Signs
of
Confrontation

Understanding Body Signs

In any face-to-face meeting there exists an almost impenetrable wall of uncertainty built on the unknown. What is in the mind of the other individual? What will they attempt to do? Will it be all verbal or will there be physical confrontation? Neither party can predict what will occur in the next few seconds.

In a momentary, sweeping glance, you must identify the key areas of the other individual's body: the eyes, the arms, the hands, and the feet. Their position can reveal what you need to know so you can prepare yourself for any personal action. Do not assume or anticipate what your opponent will do. Do not concentrate on the ravings of the mouth. Learn to understand the more complex message the body is telegraphing.

Definition of Terms

To place the concepts into a perspective that will be easier for us to understand, we will break them down into three categories; **neutral, defensive,** and **aggressive**.

Neutral - The neutral person is between the positions of defensive and aggressive. They exhibit little or no emotion. The neutral person seems almost "relaxed". Watch carefully for any changes! The body signs that signal change can be very subtle and discrete.

Defensive - The defensive person is resistant. It could be that they are resistant to you as an individual, what you have said to them, or what you have asked them to do. They could also be resistant to you simply for what you represent to them. Changes from defensive to aggressive are usually sudden. When dealing with a defensive person you should try to de-escalate the situation, so the other person's attitude goes from defensive to neutral.

Aggressive - This person is ready for action! There are occasions when a person's actions are non-threatening, but more commonly they are agitated and ready for confrontation. This confrontation can be verbal or physical in nature. Be careful when dealing with an aggressive person because verbal action often incites them to physical action. It is important to make sure your dialogue and body gestures are non-aggressive. If an individual's position is hostile or **aggressive**, continue with comments and actions that will guide the situation in the direction you select.

What the Body is Saying

The Eyes

The eyes are the pathway the mind follows. Wherever the eyes are focused, so is the mind. When a person's eyes are wide open and looking at you, this could be seen as a NEUTRAL gesture. When a person is avoiding contact with your eyes and looking all over the area around you and them, this could be seen as a DEFENSIVE gesture. When a person narrows their eyes and maintains direct eye contact with you, this could be seen as an AGGRESSIVE gesture.

Be prepared to act to protect yourself from an individual who is continually glancing at or openly staring at a specific area of your body, such as your hands or feet. They may be trying to think of a plan to take physical control of the situation away from you. Also, be prepared to act if a person is staring at a concealed area nearby - their briefcase or a desk drawer or any other area where an object might be hidden that could be used against you.

The Head

When a person's head is resting evenly in balance on their neck, this could be seen as a NEUTRAL gesture. When the person's head is leaning back, trying to create a greater distance between the two of you, this could be seen as a DEFENSIVE gesture. When a person's head is leaning forward, this could be interpreted in two ways: The individual could be seeking more information by having closer contact with you or with what you are saying. This is an example of non-confrontational aggression. They could also be trying to intimidate you. Both cases are considered AGGRESSIVE gestures because the individual wants to take some form of action.

The Arms

The position of an individual's arms can forecast possible action. Arms fully extended and hanging relaxed at a person's side generally indicate a relaxed frame of mind. When seated, the arms would be resting on the arms of the chair, or on the table in front of them. These could both be seen as NEUTRAL gestures. When a person's arms are folded across their chest, it usually denotes insecurity, fear, or defiance. This could be seen as a DEFENSIVE gesture. When the arms are tense and the elbows are bent, this raises the hands above the waist. If the person is seated, the hands will be above the table. Whether the hands are open or clenched in a fist, their arms could be considered to be in an AGGRESSIVE gesture.

The Hands

When a person's hands are open and relaxed, their arms at their sides or resting on the table in front of them, this could be considered a NEUTRAL gesture. When a person is constantly moving their fingers or shifting their hands from the table top to their lap and back again, this could be seen as a nervous or DEFENSIVE gesture.

When a person's hands are clenched into a fist or the individual is opening and closing their hand repeatedly, this is usually viewed as an AGGRESSIVE gesture.

There are times, however, when a person will be so overcome with emotion, they will clench their fists. Extreme fear causes us to tighten all muscles. If they don't have someone else to grab, an individual will pull their arms in close to their body and squeeze their hands shut as tight as possible. Extreme joy causes athletes around the world to thrust their fist up in the air in a triumphant gesture. Politicians will pump their fists to emphatically drive a point home. In all cases, the emotions are extreme and the hands are clenched in fists.

The position of the hands can also be an indication as to whether or not an individual intends to take action against you. Hands on the hips are usually DEFENSIVE or defiant, similar to arms folded across the chest. Hands behind the back can send very mixed signals. If the person has a military background, this is a signal that they are at ease in your presence and it would be a NEUTRAL gesture, however, this could also be an individual who is trying to hide something from you. Be very careful when you see hands behind the back. It is best to consider "the total picture" of body signs and weigh all of them for a more accurate interpretation.

The Feet

Whether a person is standing or seated, the feet can tell a lot about their attitude. If someone is standing with their body weight evenly distributed on both feet and neither foot is predominately forward, this could be seen as a relaxed, NEUTRAL gesture. When a person is leaning back, and the majority of their body weight is on their heels, this could be a DEFENSIVE gesture. In order to make a quick attack, an individual needs to redistribute body weight over the front area or ball of his feet. This makes them more mobile so they can run from you or lunge forward at you. When a person is leaning forward on the balls of their feet, this could be seen as an AGGRESSIVE gesture.

When a person is seated, the placement of their feet can be just as important as when they are standing. When the legs are positioned so the bottoms of both feet are on the floor and the lower legs are perpendicular to the chair, this could be a NEUTRAL gesture. When a seated person positions his feet directly between themselves and the individual they are having a dialogue with and crosses their legs above the knees, this could be a DEFENSIVE gesture. When an individual places his feet under the chair that the toe area of the foot is making contact with the floor, causing that individual to lean forward, this could be seen as an AGGRESSIVE gesture.

When you are having a dialogue or discussion with an individual and that person quickly shifts one of their feet back into a position under the chair they are sitting on, this can tell you that the person is having a change in their attitude of what is being discussed and have moved into a more aggressive position. If it is a group discussion, the individual that has been silent may be gesturing that they now want to be more active in the dialogue. Try to remember what was said to invoke this reaction for future discussions. This can help you manipulate not only the conversation, but also the attitudes of the people involved.

Another piece of information that can be determined from foot placement is whether a person is right or left handed. Usually, a person will put their "strong side" foot (right foot if they are right handed - left foot if they are left handed) further back for more power. This is an instinctive response so even if a person is not a "trained fighter" they can react in this manner. When seated, if someone becomes more aggressive in their speech or attitude, they change their footing, placing their strong side back, getting ready for action. Be very cautious if a person changes their foot position! This most always signals impending action.

It is important to remember that the most reliable and consistent method for understanding nonverbal messages is combining several body gestures. There will be times when you will see individuals who are between the categories or are displaying mixed messages. This is quite normal when you factor in all our individualities and cultural differences.

Examples of Body Signs

Example One

You are about to interview a person who is sitting in a chair with their hands open and their arms resting on the table in front of them. They are looking right at you with their eyes wide open and their head is balanced between their shoulders.

This person is?

NEUTRAL   DEFENSIVE   AGGRESSIVE

Example Two

As the interview progresses, this person starts to lean back in the chair, crosses their legs and folds their arms across their chest. Their head leans back and instead of looking at you as you speak, they start looking around the room, avoiding eye contact, even when speaking to you.

This person is?

NEUTRAL   DEFENSIVE   AGGRESSIVE

Example Three

Further into your interview, this individual starts leaning forward in their seat, with their feet under the chair and their body leaning forward. Their hands are clenched shut and their eyes are narrowed, looking right at you.

This person is?

NEUTRAL   DEFENSIVE   AGGRESSIVE

Now that you are aware of the non-verbal messages others send, it is important for you to consider the body signals you are presenting. In most situations, you should make a constant and concerted effort to display neutral body gestures. Your actions can de-escalate a situation and guide a potentially aggressive scenario to a peaceful conclusion.

What the Hands are Saying

Some people use their hands a great deal when they are talking, while others are much less animated and use their hands very little. The one thing that is consistent is that we all talk with our hands. People will even use their hands while talking when there is no one else present. Have you ever caught yourself using hand gestures while you were rehearsing a speech by yourself or talking on the telephone? Hand gestures supplement verbal communication and many times the person speaking does not realize the gestures are being used. These signals can be very informative and many times are more reliable than the words being spoken. Most hand gestures can be divided into three basic groups, displayed at different levels of intensity. They are **palm up, palm down**, and the palm facing the person being spoken to or **vertical palm**.

The **palm up** gesture is displayed a supplement to verbal conversation to emphasize the comments being presented, such as "it was a lot of work . . ." or "Wow, that's bright.". The palm up is also used when you are asking for or receiving information. Just as you turn hand palm up to receive an object, you turn your hand up to take in information. Questions such as "Do you agree?" or "Will you allow them . . ." cause us to turn our hands to a receiving position. Normally this gesture is not used with a demand or when speaking in an authoritative tone. When we are seeking cooperation and requesting information the hands are **palm up**.

The **palm down** gesture is displayed as the reverse of the palm up gesture. It is shown as a supplement to forceful conversation or added as emphasis to an order or command. The words that accompany this hand signal are usually blunt and precise such as "Get out of the office!" or "We will be at that meeting.". A statement made with direct verbal force usually includes other body signs as well as the hand gestures. When a person points their finger, even though most of the fingers are folded back, when this motion is being done for emphasis or to demand action, the palm is down.

The **vertical palm** is the universal "stop sign". Whether it is an index finger on the lips to silently ask someone to stop talking or an arm extended with the palm displayed to tell a motorist to stop his vehicle, the message is clear. The individual using this gesture is in a position to regulate the flow of the actions or conversation taking place and something must cease.

The **vertical palm** is a commonly displayed gesture in a meeting or group situation. The person who utilizes this gesture is assuming the position of leader and will try to maintain control of others involved. It is important to observe the level of intensity or how emphatically this gesture is displayed. This information can tell you the amount of authority the person has in that group. If a person achieves control with a slight and rather relaxed gesture, this individual is one who has command of the scene without the need to "over display." This person is also more apt to be quiet in their speech and in control of all around them.

If, however, the reverse is true and you are observing someone with a lower confidence level who is trying to appear more impressive and important to those around them, most of the body gestures and especially the hand gestures will become more bold and flagrant. The volume level also becomes pronounced and the words themselves more staccato.

When you observe a group of people from a distance and cannot hear what is being said, hand gestures can be an important means of obtaining knowledge of the situation. Who is giving the orders? Who is asking for direction? is anyone in the group more agitated? If you can be more aware of what you are about to encounter, you will have better control of the situation and lessen the possibility of aggression against you.

Extreme Circumstances

If you are in contact with a person who has been subjected to physical or mental torture you will usually perceive a drastically altered response. People who have been beaten or severely injured can become totally drained or "bleached" of all normal body signs, both aggressive and defensive.

Movies, television, and the entertainment industry have given us a false image of the normal response of a person who has been emotionally devastated by an incident or event. They often display the person as being extremely "hyper", overly expressive, and at a high level of reactive gestures. In most cases, this will not be true. You will notice that the response to any questioning will be extremely diminished. They will usually display little if any emotion, even to questions that should normally evoke an aggressive response. All accompanying hand and facial gestures will be muted. They will appear to be exhausted and depleted of energy. They appear to be without emotion when, in reality, they are in deep need of professional care that should be encouraged without delay.

When a person has been a victim of an extreme circumstance, they rarely show open hostility toward their abuser. Open displays and threats against an aggressor are usually made by an interested third party, not the victim.

The few body signs that will surface on a person who has been tortured or witnessed an incident of torture first hand will normally be neutral gestures. The level of gestures will usually be at a consistent level - no ups or downs. There will be little change of expression or emotion throughout your entire dialogue. Most of the information you will amass will be through observation and not interaction.

Part Two

Interactive
Dialogue

The Conversational Distance

Imagine that, between you and the person to whom you are speaking, there is a space into which your words fit. During most conversations, the entire dialogue takes place with one, established distance from the start of the discussion to its end. But when the emotional level changes, so does the space between those involved.

Various cultures have different amounts or degrees of "personal space". What is important for us to observe is not the distance a conversation begins at, but the fluctuations of the distances between the parties while they are talking. This will give us a better understanding of the dynamics of the dialogue as we see it unfold before us. It will help us understand the importance of what has been said.

When a person is **aggressive** or has strong emotional feelings about what is being said, they will lean forward, to compress the area their words have to travel. Also, when the item being discussed is of a personal or private nature, the person will have a tendency to lean into their words.

When a person is speaking, but is **defensive**, and thinks their comments will be met with a negative reaction, many times they will anticipate the aggressive response by leaning or stepping back as they speak to avoid having the conversational distance compressed. If they feel their comments will be met with a positive response, they will lean forward or step in closer in anticipation of acceptance of their point of view.

When two individuals meet, the contact distance that quickly becomes established can tell us more than the verbal greetings being exchanged. If two people have had prior contact that was of a negative nature, the distance between them will be greater than the distance established between two friends. Another reliable body gesture that often accompanies this is whether or not the eyes narrow as the individuals extend their arms for a handshake or other traditional greeting. Narrowed eyes are a sign that the person being met is not being accepted or possibly trusted.

The Volume Factor

The volume of our speech can be a vital key to our emotional state. Many times, we react to volume keys without even realizing it. Consider the common phrases we all use in our daily lives - "three cheers for the winner", or "a moment of silence, please". The circumstance in which a person perceives themselves to be will a major contributing factor to the volume and pitch of their voice.

Be aware of any subtle changes in the volume, speed, or pitch of a person's voice as they speak. It can reveal what they feel is of greater importance to the circumstance at hand. The volume generated by a person in a conversation with one or more other persons will rise and fall in direct proportion to how important they think their comments are to the meeting.

When a person is **aggressive**, they will raise their voice and become louder. This can be to emphasize a point in a discussion or it can be in the form of a shout to a friend across a crowded room.

When an individual is agitated or emotional, the speech will not only become louder, it will also become faster. When a person is seeking to achieve control of the situation, the language of the dialogue will become louder but the cadence will usually slow down and become more deliberate.

When a person is **defensive**, the volume can be more subdued or quiet. Their cadence will usually be slower, as if they are thinking about every word before they say it. A common defensive speech pattern is when someone mumbles. This is slowing the words and dropping the volume to a point where the words become inaudible.

What we must seek to do, under most circumstances, is to keep our volume level consistent. When needed, yield the floor to those who are eager to "tip their hand" with comments they never intended to make. Whether it is a social gathering or a business conference, be aware of not just what is being said, but how it is being said. The hidden meanings can be of great value to you when trying to assess the situation.

Confrontational Positioning

Confrontational Positioning refers to the stance and body placement an individual assumes when coming into contact with one or more other persons. The positioning that is taken can display safety status of yourself or others, authority level, or acceptance within the structural group.

When a person or group of people is willing to accept you and they are in a non-confrontational position, they will face you and be toward the front of your body so you can see them. If you observe a group of people from a distance and everyone seems to be facing one individual, that person is probably the "leader" of the group. At that point in time, that person has the most authority and influence on the activities of that group.

When a group of people is not willing to accept someone into their trust or if the situation is escalating into an aggressive condition, the people will try to encompass the "outsider". This will limit that individual's ability to monitor everyone else's actions. It will make the group feel superior and more in control. If you are in a situation where you feel a group of individuals is trying to establish an aggressive position behind your back or out of your view, try to physically step back, keeping the majority of the group where they can be observed for any action against you.

Just as with animals, humans will try to protect the weak and the old by placing them in the center of the group. An important person or someone with authority will also be protected by the gathering. Do not assume the person at the head of the crowd is the one who is in charge. Watch the body signs of the rest of the people to determine who is the most important one.

The Friendly Attack

Why do people compromise what was once a totally inflexible demand? Why do they suddenly yield to a different point of view or request? Could it be that we all place a higher priority on the body signs we see in others than we realize? Can these gestures be used to help us achieve our goals?

When an individual is involved in a form of personal contact with others, whether it is casual and random, or well planned but difficult, our body signs clearly reflect the intent and substance of the words being spoken. If we are to successfully manipulate the dialogue, we need to learn how to control body signs and "say" what we want with discrete gestures.

When a person is displaying **neutral** body gestures, they will be open to suggestions and willing to compromise. When the body gestures become **defensive**, even if it appears that they are listening to what you are saying, their mind could be busy thinking of strategies to stop you from changing their mind and they may not be receptive to your ideas. When a person is aggressive, they will go beyond being close minded and demand their own way. They can be so caught up in the moment that they will refuse your suggestion, even when it is simply a restatement of their own demand, such as a person refusing a half dozen pieces of something because they demanded six of them.

When a person is in a defensive or aggressive posture, do not expect them to change their way of thinking to your ideas. They need to relax their state of mind to be open to new concepts. When a person is defensive, they are usually trying to think of a counter measure to what you are proposing. This is the time the discussion can be swayed off the main topic to side issues that are irrelevant. Be careful not to be lead off course or to let your gestures take the deliberations in a direction they need not go.

How do we keep people neutral and receptive to our concepts? We must remain neutral ourselves. Allow the other side to speak its mind but make sure your body signs remain neutral, even if your emotions do not. After they have stated what they want, they will see your gestures and be more likely to remain neutral and open to your ideas. If your reactions become defensive, they will become defensive, and the entire discussion will become mired down in negative feelings. Instead of working towards a compromise, both sides will become frustrated with the situation.

You can only feed your requests to someone who is willing to listen to them. By continuing to display neutral body signs, you lessen the tendency of the others to slip into a defensive state of body gestures, and allow for an environment where they will be more susceptible to the perspective you are placing before them.

Part Three

Manipulating
Dialogue

Control
Are You In Control?

To be blunt, we need to maintain control. We must control our emotions, our actions and the situations in which we are involved. Remember, even a mob has a leader. We need to stay focused and well grounded no matter what is occurring around us. We cannot seek to control or manipulate the other side of the conversation if we do not have control in our own team. The leadership of the team of which you are apart must be better than the leadership that is presented across the table from you.

Control can take place in many forms. It can be extremely subtle and discrete, such as controlling the temperature of the room or the time of the meeting to better suit your personal needs. Control can be blatantly obvious, even to the point of being insulting and dictatorial. Maintain control, but do not cause the opposition to become defensive and unresponsive.

Control the direction of the interactive dialogue. Guide the participants in the appropriate direction to seek out a solution to the problem that brought you and/or your teams together. Always remember, we can talk about having a balance of authority and decision making power in mediation and negotiation situations, but when you have a certain objective or goal, it is preferable to have that balance in your favor. Discrete control can achieve this goal without offending the other groups involved.

The organization and leadership skills you display by maintaining personal control will help your team achieve its goals and keep the discussion focused on the objectives that need to be addressed.

The Agenda
Better Yours Than Theirs

Do not be confused or frightened by the word "agenda". To put this concept into a simple definition, think of it as a list of things that both sides of a deliberation want to openly discuss at the meeting table. The list may be extremely brief or it can be quite extensive and involved.

Whether a relationship is predicated on a written document or a casual handshake, it needs to be carefully developed and reinforced with trust. Great care should be taken to make sure any list or agenda contains items that are of interest to all concerned. This will help to ensure that everyone will become involved in the meeting and negotiations.

Be aware of the basic concept of the "good vs. bad" agenda. Simply put - our agenda is good for us—their agenda is good for them which could make it bad for us. This perspective may seem a bit ruthless or downright inconsiderate at first glance, but it is important to hold to your own perspective throughout the negotiations. Be careful not to win ground at the bargaining table only to loose footing at the final agreement.

Respectfully solicit written items for an agenda. Encourage both sides of any negotiation to feel that they are an equal part of the meeting and process. Remember though, that whenever you put something in writing and give it to someone else, there is a good chance you will have to live with it. However, and quite properly so, when the opposition puts something forward in its written agenda, they too can be held accountable.

The Other Team
Basic Personality Types
You May Encounter

Amid the vast multitude of people we will have the pleasure and total displeasure of dealing with, no two will be the same. Because we are all somewhat human, we are also unique in every facet of our lives and experiences. We do, however, have certain similarities and common traits when we interact with others. Keeping this in mind, let us examine some of the generalized types of individuals we could encounter and how they might interact with us.

The Enthusiastic Misdirector

This is a person who generally appears to be highly self-motivated and interested in every word spoken by any and all people. They have the tendency to be overly interactive with comments and questions and, with total spontaneity, they can, and will, take over the meeting or conversation by providing an endless flood of commentary. They classically will talk more and more about less and less until they have said everything there is to say about nothing.

Body Signs

The Enthusiastic Misdirector will exhibit wide open eyes that seem to spend more time rambling around the room than making direct eye contact with whomever is speaking. They generally are leaning forward in their chair in anticipation of adding to the discussion. Their arms will be resting on the table or placed in their lap in a relaxed manner. They spend most of their time speaking with their palms up, directing their comments to everyone in the area in a routine manner. They do not acknowledge anyone as an authority or team leader.

Solution

There is no polite, socially acceptable, or otherwise gracious way to intercede in this onslaught of verbal commentary, so just interrupt. As long as it is done with a smile on your face and a "thank you for bringing that up", or "Let's get back to OUR agenda", you can usually regain control without offending the Misdirector. You can compliment them **but** make sure you display aggressive gestures to show control while doing it. You may have to become quite assertive with these gestures - even confusing the Misdirector by displaying aggressive gestures when stating neutral comments. If it becomes a severe problem, call for a brief recess. After the break, guide the meeting back in the direction it needs to go by immediately setting forth a new proposal or refer back to the agenda. The main point is that you must maintain control of the meeting and keep it going in a direction that will benefit your team.

The Quiet Ambusher

This is the person who sits back throughout the meeting and lets others make statements, as questions, and develop the strengths and openings for their side during the debate process. They may or may not be diligently taking notes in a physical manner but be assured that they are quite aware of the topics and direction of the conversation. Some ambushers are interested in the entire dialogue of the meeting, however, most will be lying in wait for the moment their area of concern or topic of interest is introduced and commented on. Remember one extremely important trait about the ambusher - they seldom ask any questions to which they do not already know the answers! Their interest in this meeting is strictly to catch you off guard in a mistake or a lie. Their efforts are not to be dealt with lightly or brushed aside.

Body Signs

The Quiet Ambusher will sit back in silence, making direct eye contact with everyone who speaks. The head movement will be limited, but the eye movement will be in a constant state of scanning all who offer a comment. Whether they are studiously leaning forward on the table, or in a relaxed "lean back in the chair" manner, in most cases, they will be taking notes on the conversation. One of the most unusual gestures this person will display is that they will ask a question with their palms down. We have said that this gesture is usually used to show force or direct a statement. Do not be confused by what appears to be a shift in displayed gestures. The words may be phrased in the form of a question but there is a definite statement being made. This forceful question can become a focal point or a major problem if not handled properly.

Solution

It is the nature of the Quiet Ambusher to gather strength and power from your mistakes. Their greatest power and ultimate goal is to catch you trying to cover up the inaccuracies or conflicts you make in your presentation and comments. If you are caught in a mistake that you can admit to and still survive the meeting, it is best, in most cases, to do just that. The mistake or untruth you side step and do not directly address will have a tendency to come back and haunt you at the most inopportune moments.

Make sure your body signs remain neutral at all times. If you display defensive gestures when admitting to a mistake, the Quiet Ambusher will "dig deeper" to try to find more errors. If you become aggressive, they have achieved their goal and you have lost control of the situation. In both cases, your credibility has been destroyed and your team's agenda has been compromised. Stay neutral.

If "the worst thing" happens and you find yourself in what appears to be an error, you have a limited range of temporary damage control techniques or relatable comments. "Let me get back to you on that point", or "let's get back to the agenda" may pacify the opposition for a brief while. If the debate starts to become heated, ask for a brief recess. If the confrontation seems to be aimed at one member of your team in a more personal manner, it may be best to have that member "called away" and replace them for the remainder of the conference.

The Meeting Interviewer

This person is more of an annoyance than the clever tactical problem the other types presented. The main negative contribution this person can provide is that if your side pays attention to this distractor, they will not be able to pay attention to the agenda and issues of the meeting.

The Meeting Interviewer can not only be a problem for your team, but for the other party of negotiators as well. There are several unfortunate traits that this "legend in their own mind" poses. One of the things they relish doing is being in charge of reading and, unfortunately, rereading the agenda. At any moment the entire conference room can be thrown into a yawning fit by the individual saying, "Let's look at this again . . .". Perhaps one of the most time consuming and boring efforts they make is the constant and incessant repeating of everything that is said. It is, of course, preceded by a comment such as "Let's see if I understand you" or "Oh! You mean . . .", and the list can go on and on . . . The only thing this person is missing is the background music and spotlight for the full enhancement of the unique abilities they think they have.

The amount of contribution this person makes to the meeting is minimal. There are times however, when a "Quiet Ambusher" from the other side will encourage this interviewer because as you become more aggravated with their repetitious behavior, you are more apt to make changes and errors in your statements.

Body Signs

The Meeting Interviewer is deeply involved in the debate process and generally will focus their full attention on the person who is talking at all times, even if the person is on their side of the table. It is not unusual for their own team members to gesture to this individual to be quiet. Hand and eye motions will show they are equally annoyed with the interruptions. The Interviewer will usually be leaning forward at the table with wide eyes, constantly turning to face anyone that speaks. The majority of hand gestures displayed by this person will be flamboyant and palm up, asking and/or repeating everything said.

Solution

The solution to the problem the Interviewer presents is not difficult, but it is a team problem and requires a team solution. All group members must be consistent and state similar comments when challenged by this distraction. Politely but forcefully state, "Please don't interrupt my chain of thought", "Please wait until I am finished", "Please don't repeat what I have just said", or "It is a waste of OUR time to read that again". Notice, all of the above phrases are statements. We have not asked them to comment on anything. This would only give them the opportunity they are looking for to continue domination of the conversation. The goal we are seeking to achieve is their silence. The team's body gestures should remain aggressive toward the Meeting Interviewer, much in the same manner as it should be toward the Misdirector. You may not need as many comments to control the Meeting Interviewer, but the level of intensity may have to be more forceful.

Dialogue to "The Authority"
Who Do You Talk To?

Your time and effort will always be best spent when dealing with the person who is "in charge" of the meeting or conference you are attending. You do not want to be placed in the position of dealing with an assistant or a person who is second in command of any negotiations. Take control of the situation by manipulating or reading the physical signs that are being displayed by the other side and use them to your advantage.

The unofficial rules of "talk and respond" are established in the first few minutes of any contact with another person or group. If you have been advised through formal introduction or procedure as to who is in charge of the opposing team or group, then it is to your advantage to focus on that person directly. No matter which member of the other side asks your team a question, your response is directed to the person who is leading the other team. All of your team's responses and questions should be directed at this one individual.

To diffuse the opposition's verbal attack on your team, whenever a question is asked, it should be answered by different members of your team on an almost rotating basis. This will help keep the other team off balance and not allow them the comfort of knowing who is leading your group.

If the leader of the opposition is not introduced to you, the other side is making an effort to present a wall of defense to limit your level of effectiveness in the interchange, then you must try to determine who is in charge so your team has a focal person. Trying to determine the leadership of the other side during the actual meeting can be rather difficult. Try to be prepared for the meeting early, and discretely observe the individuals who will be involved. This will allow you the opportunity of seeing the opposition in their unguarded moments. In any case, make note of who the other team is facing when they are talking. Are they standing, or are the chairs arranged, so they are facing one person? Which speakers are talking with their palms up and who is the one figure who is instructing the others with a palm down gesture? The actual conversation being spoken is not as important as the body signs they are giving you. You now know the individual they have chosen to be their leader for this meeting.

Be aware that the leadership role can appear to change during a discussion. If the subject matter diverts to a technical specialty, a member of the opposing team who is more qualified to answer those questions may try to step in and become the authority. Do not be swayed or lead off course. Continue to address the original leader as they will ultimately be the one to retain control.

When approaching the conference table, a good diversionary tactic for your team is to have it appear as if you have divided the leadership role. If the opposition has no one person to target, their attack will be defused on your entire team, thus making it stronger.

This method of attack and counter attack is really quite simple. Your group focuses on one member of their team, and their efforts are defused on all the individuals of your team evenly. Your force and efforts are strongest when focused on one person or area of attack. A chain can bear great stress, but it was not designed to have one link bear the entire load.

What Do They Really Want
Watching for the Subtle Signals

You are sitting in your "vehicle of conversation" at the "spotlight of interactive dialogue", watching the signals change, and not knowing when to proceed. Let us start to put together what we have learned and apply it to the question of "what do they really want?".

As you and your fellow colleagues sit in uncertainty, watching the opposition, you will begin to notice some subtle and discrete signals that are now quite apparent to you. As their focus person, or group leader, begins to speak, you will become aware that you have a new methodology for understanding the "unspoken conversation" that is about to take place in front of you.

Visualize a picture of several members of a team sitting across from you at a meeting table. Some are fumbling through papers for notes they forgot to take. Another, looking up with a pencil in his mouth, is thinking about the vacation that is only three weeks away. And one other person, the focus leader, is reading off a list of request and demands that you are now intently trying to concentrate on. As the list progresses, you are wondering which of these items is the most important and what you should be concentrating most of your energy toward. Which items are negotiable requests and which items are polite demands ... and then, all of a sudden, you know! How did they convey this information to you? The waterfall of subtle signals said more than their spoken word.

As the person was reading off their list of items, you noticed a difference in the "whole person" by being aware of their involuntary expression changes and gestures. As the leader began to read a certain demand or request, you noticed a slight palm up gesture being displayed. They wanted your immediate approval of that item. You also noticed that the leader leaned forward in their chair and spoke just slightly louder as that point was presented. Their intent was quite clear. This was the item of greatest importance to them. Now your team was able to devise a strategy around this insight, and use this knowledge to better manipulate the discussion.

What if the opposite situation is occurring? What if you are the person reading off a list of demands and you want to know how the other team is going to accept your ideas? Which items will be agreed upon and which items will be met with resistance? Let us consider this scenario. You are reading along through your "wish list" of demands and requests when you come to an item that causes an obvious shift in body gestures from three out of the four people sitting across the table from you. The first person leans back in their chair and folds their arms across their chest. This is the classic defensive posture and this individual has just told you he does not agree with you on that issue. Another person on the other team shifts his body position toward his own leader and displays wide eyes and palms up. This person is not sure of how they should feel and they are asking the leader to direct their thinking. The leader hears what you have read and leans back. Not only do they fold their arms across their chest, they also cross their legs above the knees and narrow their eyes as they glare at their own associates. This person is saying that not only are they opposed to what has just been said, they want their team-mates to be opposed to it too.

You must also be aware of the body gestures of members on your own team when you are in negotiation or confer-ence setting. When you are in an intense verbal debate and you see an esteemed colleague look at the clock and let out a quiet sign as they lean back, looking up at the ceiling, they have just told you, loud and clear, that they are through with this part of the meeting and whatever else is discussed means very little to them at this point in time.

Remember, as you read others, they are reading you. Body gestures can develop and change very quickly. Stay alert to the nonverbal communication that is occurring around you.

The Gesture Mirror
Using Natural Reactions

When we are exposed to certain circumstances, we react in a very consistent and predictable manner. How many times have you started laughing with everyone else even though you had no idea what was funny? Have you ever tried not to yawn when someone else did? People have a tendency to become a part of what is happening around them, and there is in all of us, an acute susceptibility to the "contagion of gestures."

This gesture mirror can be used to your advantage if you are aware of it. If you are in a negotiation setting and you are having a difficult time with one of the members of the opposing team, watch that individual during your breaks or at times when the conditions are neutral. What do they do when they are relaxed? Is there a certain phrase or gesture they use when they are happy or cheerful? Is there any information you can gather that will make them more sympathetic to your cause or agenda? What body signs tell you they are relaxed and open to new concepts?

When you are presenting a new item and you want them to agree with you, use their neutral gestures. Unconsciously, this will lessen their defenses and make them more open to your ideas. Bring up items you have in common and that are of concern to everyone. Use their gestures to present these ideas as well. When you finally state your demands, these borrowed gestures can make them think the concepts presented were, at least in part, their own idea.

Reacting To Displayed Gestures
Your Quiet Control

Going nowhere at top speed? Are you working hard at a meeting where you and your team feel like you are talking to people who are about as receptive as a brick wall? You just might be talking to a wall - a wall of opposition. You are trying to communicate with individuals who have constructed a barrier of body gestures to block you out. As long as they sit there unchallenged and unchanged, they will not agree to anything you present. You need to guide your team into open and receptive gestures to get through the wall of anti-communication.

Why did the other group of negotiators become defensive so quickly? Your notes and papers are spread out all over in front of you, your arms are on the table and you're leaning forward in your seat. Your eyes are narrow and your gaze is fixed on the opposition leader. You are ready for battle. And a battle is just what you will get. The other group is leaning back in their seats, their arms are crossed and folded against their chests. They are looking down or around the room, anywhere so they don't have to make eye contact with you.

When we put all the body signs in writing it becomes obvious at how aggressive our team appears to be. If not out of intimidation, the other team must act defensively just for survival. Any chance of interactive dialogue is lost.

How different would the situation be if we were to approach the bargaining table in a more relaxed manner? We still must be prepared and vigilant about our agenda but it is important to display a calm demeanor. We need to manipulate the other side into a gesture display that will entice them into the discussion, making it more beneficial for everyone. Lean back in your chair and make sure your arm gestures remain neutral. Keep your eye contact and facial expressions neutral but friendly. Slowly, you will see the members of the other team start to lean forward and enter into the discussion.

Do not expect an instant response from the opposition. It will take a little time for them to start to feel comfortable with you and your team, but slowly their wall of defense will start to crumble, and their body gestures will become more open or even aggressive.

If you have had previous contact or are familiar with a member of the other group and had a good relationship with them, their defensive posturing will usually break down faster. If the contact you had was of a negative nature, it may be longer before they take you back into their confidence.

The contents of the conversation in the beginning of a negotiation are of little importance. The main concern is that the other side of the table is open to your ideas and has been successfully lured into the dialogue they were resistant to. Encourage both sides to stay active throughout the negotiations to prevent the wall of defense from being rebuilt.

The Room
A Conducive Environment

Most rooms are designed for a specific purpose such as dining, sleeping, or conducting business. You can usually walk into a room and, without being told, ascertain the purpose and the mood of the room by the furniture and its arrangement. In any negotiation or debate type setting, the mood of the room is just as important as the dialogue being presented.

Why do we consider some rooms "formal" and cold while others seem friendly and relaxed even before a word has been said? It is extremely important to keep the mood of the room you are using for a discussion neutral and "open" if you want an interactive dialogue to take place. We need to achieve a balance of perceived power between all people involved and remove the barriers that can cause defensive posturing.

If a room is arranged so that one individual is positioned behind a large, formidable desk with an oversized chair and the other person is ushered to a small chair with no furniture around it, you can be sure the dialogue will be very one sided. Information will be "extracted" and orders will be given instead of ideas and concepts being shared. If intimidation and a one way flow of speech is your goal, this office is perfect for your needs. The only thing missing is a bright light shining in the subject's eyes and cigar smoke blown in their face.

If you plan to have discussions in an office, make sure there is an area that is less formal, and where they are comfortable chairs of similar size. Let it be a more relaxed setting where the visitor will be at ease and willing to "share". If a person intimidated by their surroundings, they will not be open to participation in any form of dialogue with someone they perceive to be an authority figure.

There is little difference between two people and two teams trying to have an exchange of ideas. Always consider the other group as a single entity. This will help you concentrate on the task before you, and assist in removing the distractions of the multiple personalities across the table from you.

How can we set up a conference room for a proactive state of dialogue? Start by making sure the balance of power appears to be equal. Remove all articles such as banners or flags that are obvious stumbling blocks to open dialogue and defensive attitudes. The chairs should be comfortable and equal in all ways possible for both groups. The lighting should be bright enough for all participants to see, but not glaring. Rooms that are too dark cause emotions to become sullen and subdued. The table should be large enough to provide adequate surface area for the needed papers and related materials. Try to make sure it is not too wide. If a person from one side of the meeting is trying to share papers with an individual from the other team, they must be able to reach across the table without getting to their feet. When a person has to stand up when everyone else around them is sitting, it puts them in a very uncomfortable position. Some individuals will not participate at all if this circumstance occurs. There is little difference between intimidating conversation and inaccessible documents.

Do your best to eliminate distractions. Get rid of the clocks and telephones in the room, and turn off your pagers. If the meeting is to be perceived as important, then you need to remove the interruptions within your control. As stated earlier, do not look at your watch if it can be avoided. If the meeting has time restraints, have an individual who is not involved in the negotiations be responsible for informing the group when the meeting is ending.

Make sure there are prearranged breaks in the sessions for human needs. This will help keep the mood of the negotiations from becoming more tense as the stomachs become more empty. It will also give your team time to confer for strategic purposes and allow you to reorganize if necessary. Do not be opposed to having food or drink available during the meeting. This does help keep people in a more open state of mind.

Conclusion
A Time for Advice

You have been introduced into the incredible world of understanding others at an enhanced level. The pages you have just read are not merely concepts and ideas. They are truly alive in each and every one of us and have been a part of our lives even before we could speak. They remain with us as a viable form of communication even when we become incapacitated or infirmed.

When using these skills, remember to personally display relaxed and neutral body signs when dealing with others. Be attentive to what is being said and realize that certain concessions may have to be made in any negotiation scenario. As long as these compromises are not in direct conflict with your position, be it individual or as a group, the requests should be considered. This will help the deliberations from becoming stagnant and avoid having the conversation becoming one sided.

In order to successfully manipulate dialogue, we need to be able to instill in others the perspectives and objectives that are important to our position. We need to remember what causes negative posturing from the opposition and avoid or eliminate further gestures that can create a defensive position.

Bear in mind that the skills you have learned need to be practiced and developed. Just as a child takes many practice steps before he or she can run, it will take time for you to perceive all the *Unspoken Dialogue* that is around us every day.

To order additional copies
please use the order form
on the next page.

ORDER FORM

Telephone: 913-385-2034 *Have your credit card information ready.*

Fax: 913-385-2039

Online: www.varropress.com

Postal: Varro Press, Inc.
           P.O. Box 8413
           Shawnee Mission, Kansas (KS) USA 66208

Qty. _____ @ $12.95 each $ _____

Shipping: *
First book $5.00 $ _____
Additional copies $1.00 each $ _____

TOTAL $ _____

* Priority shipping or foreign: *Call 913-385-2034 or visit us online at varropress.com*

Ordered By:
Name: _____
Address: _____
City: _____ State _____ ZIP: _____
Country: _____
Telephone: _____

Ship To: *(If different from above.)*
Name: _____
Address: _____
City: _____ State _____ ZIP: _____
Country: _____
Telephone: _____

Payment:
☐ Check
☐ Credit Card
     ☐ VISA   ☐ MasterCard   ☐ AMEX   ☐ Discover
Card Number: _____ Exp. Date: _____
Name on Card: _____
Signature: _____

"THE UNSPOKEN DIALOGUE"

High-Impact Skills For Understanding Body Language & Controlling Dialogue, Interviews, and Negotiations

While peoples' voices are saying one thing, their body language reveals the true story of what they are secretly thinking and what they intend to do physically.

The eyes, the head, the arms, the hands, and even the feet are involuntary and undeniable pathways to revealing and understanding other people. If you learn how to "read" these signs, you'll be equipped to instantly recognize, understand, and act on the tell-tale behavior that reveals what people cannot hide. If you know what to look for, and what it means, you'll have solid, reliable, and actionable information about how to interact with, control, and even negotiate with others to your advantage.

Based on his extensive observation, study and organizational work around the world, Dr. Robert Rail has perfected his discoveries and transformed them into methods that are quick and easy to learn in his high-impact interactive skills learning sessions. Dr. Rail's "Understanding Body Language" skills are useful up and down any organization, and in every industry.

You will learn:
- What body language gestures to look for and what they mean.
- How to discover what is really being said during interactive dialogue.
- How you can control and manipulate dialogue, meetings, interviews, and negotiations with individuals and groups to your advantage.

Dr. Rail is recognized internationally as one of the foremost trainers and advisors on human behavior. His programs have been used extensively by the U.S. Department of Justice, the U.S. Department of State, NATO, the Organization for Security & Cooperation in Europe (OSCE), the United Nations Police Task Force, universities, international corporations and other organizations in the U.S, Europe, Asia, and Africa. The second edition of his book *The Unspoken Dialogue: Understanding Body Language & Controlling Interviews & Negotiations* is due out in late 2008.

For more information about customized learning sessions at your location, contact:

Michael Nossaman
Varro Press, Inc.
Tel: 913-385-2034 or michael@varro.com